This book belongs to:

_____

The Spirit in Football

GALATIANS
5:22-23

Written and Illustrated by
Kathryn Nixon and Ana Boudreau

The Spirit in Sports Publishing

Copyright 2010
ISBN: 978-0-615-38669-0
The Spirit in Baseball / Kathryn Nixon and Ana Boudreau
Published by The Spirit in Sports Publishing
Printed in China by Toppan Leefung Printing Limited

We want to dedicate this book to:

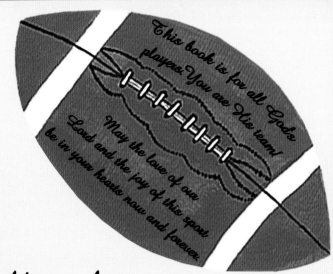

This book is for all God's players. You are His team!

May the love of our Lord and the joy of this sport be in your hearts now and forever.

Our precious children, whose spirit and passion for God's gift of sports inspire us every day.

"Children are a gift from God, they are His reward!"
Psalm 127:3

We remain grateful and humbled by the support we have received from our family, friends, and community whose passion for <u>The Spirit in Baseball</u> encouraged us to continue this amazing journey through the sport of football.

Thank you for continuing to inspire us to share God's fruit of the Spirit in <u>The Spirit in Football</u>.

It is with great excitement and joy that we expand God's playing field with you!

Blessings,
Kathryn & Ana

A Special Thank You To:

Our beloved husbands, Trot Nixon and Mark Boudreau, for their constant support, and to our entire families for their encouragement and prayers.

Chase Nixon
Luke Nixon
Julia Boudreau
Katherine Boudreau
Lauren Boudreau
Ivy Zingone
Kathryn Zingone
Matthew Finley

Kim Olinger
Kenny Dickerson and SEAM Ministries
Norm and Bobbe Evans
Brent Coeling
Sarah Hasselbeck
Photographs provided by Seattle Seahawks

And to:
Matt Hasselbeck whose life on and off the field exemplifies the virtues of the fruit of the Spirit through the game of football.

"The fruits of the Spirit are essential in being a good teammate and a good sport. In sports it is important to be as driven and competitive as possible; however, that drive and competitiveness should never come before obeying the rules and being a good sport. These lessons are true in athletics no matter what sport or level you're competing."

Matt Hasselbeck

NFL Professional Quarterback

Just as our Heavenly Father hides the
"fruit of the Spirit" within our hearts, we have hidden
God's created fruit for you to seek throughout this book.

"But the fruit of the Spirit is love, joy, peace, patience, kindness, goodness, faithfulness,
gentleness and self-control"

Galatians 5:22-23

The Spirit in Football

Love
As we huddle together before each game, we lovingly encourage each other in prayer. God wants us to play the best we can to honor Him.
Hebrews 10:24 "Think of ways to encourage one another with outbursts of love and good deeds."

Joy
The fans cheered with excitement and joy as our team scored the first touchdown of the game.
Job 8:21 "He will fill your mouth with laughter and your lips with shouts of joy."

Peace
We play football with a strong desire to win. We are filled with passion and peace in our heart knowing we are play for the glory of God.
Psalm 34:14 "Turn away from evil and do good. Work hard at living in peace with others."

Patience
Our coaches are patient with us as we learn offensive and defensive plays.
1 Thessalonians 5:14 "Encourage those who are timid. Take care of those who are weak. Be patient with everyone."

Kindness
Even if I fumble the ball or make an incomplete pass, my teammates support me and treat me with kindness and respect.
Ephesians 4:32 "Be kind to each other, tenderhearted, forgiving one another, just as God through Christ has forgiven you."

Goodness
We should always be good to one another. We should show compassion and comfort to a teammate or opponent who is hurt.
Romans 12:9 "Don't just pretend to love others. Really love them. Hate what is wrong. Hold tightly to what is good."

Faithfulness
To be a good football player we have to practice our plays faithfully. To love God we must practice serving Him faithfully.
Joshua 22:5 "Love the Lord your God, walk in all His ways, obey His commands, be faithful to Him, and serve Him with all your heart and soul."

Gentleness
If we are upset about a penalty, instead of acting out in anger, God calls us to react with gentleness and respect.
Proverbs 15:1 "A gentle answer deflects anger, but harsh words make tempers flare."

Self-control
We must show self-control by not losing our temper when we are tackled aggressively by the other team.
2 Timothy 1:7 "God did not give us a Spirit of fear, but of power, of love and of self-control."

LOVE

"Think of ways to encourage one another with outbursts of *Love* and good deeds."

Hebrews 10:24

As we huddle together before each game, we *Lovingly* encourage each other in prayer. God wants us to play the best we can to honor Him.

"He will fill your mouth with laughter and your lips with shouts of *Joy*."

Job 8:21

PEACE

"Turn away from evil and do good.
Work hard at living in *Peace*
with others."

Psalm 34:14

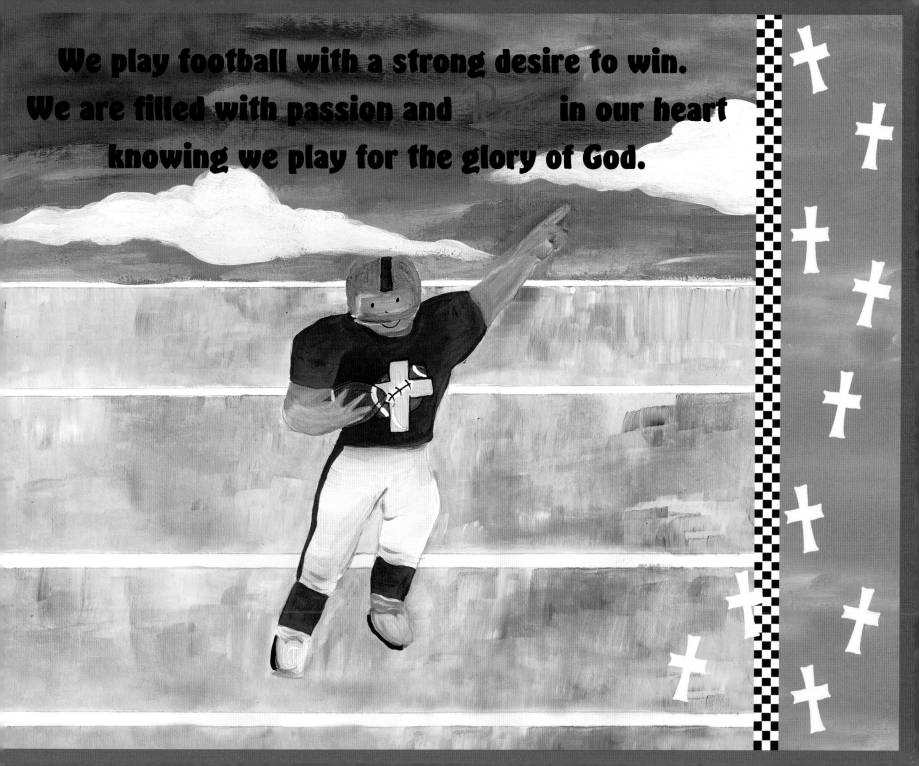

PATIENCE

"Encourage those who are timid. Take care of those who are weak. Be *Patient* with everyone."

1 Thessalonians 5:14

Our coaches are *Patient* with us as
we learn offensive and defensive plays.

"Be Kind to each other, tenderhearted, forgiving one another, just as God through Christ has forgiven you."

Ephesians 4:32

Even if I fumble the ball or make an incomplete pass, my teammates support me and treat me with Kindness and respect.

"Don't just pretend to love others.
Really love them.
Hate what is wrong.
Hold tightly to what is *Good*."

Romans 12:9

We should always be Good to one another. We should show compassion and comfort to a teammate or opponent who is hurt.

FAITHFULNESS

"Love the Lord your God, walk in all His ways, obey His commands, be Faithful to Him, and serve Him with all your heart and soul."

Joshua 22:5

To be a good football player we have to practice our plays Faithfully. To love God we must practice serving Him Faithfully.

"A Gentle answer deflects anger,
but harsh words make tempers flare."

Proverbs 15:1

If we are upset about a penalty, instead of acting out in anger, God calls us to react with Gentleness and respect.

"God did not give us a Spirit of fear,
but of power, of love and of *Self-control*."

2 Timothy 1:7

We must show Self-control by not losing our temper when we are tackled aggressively by the other team.

Mission Statement

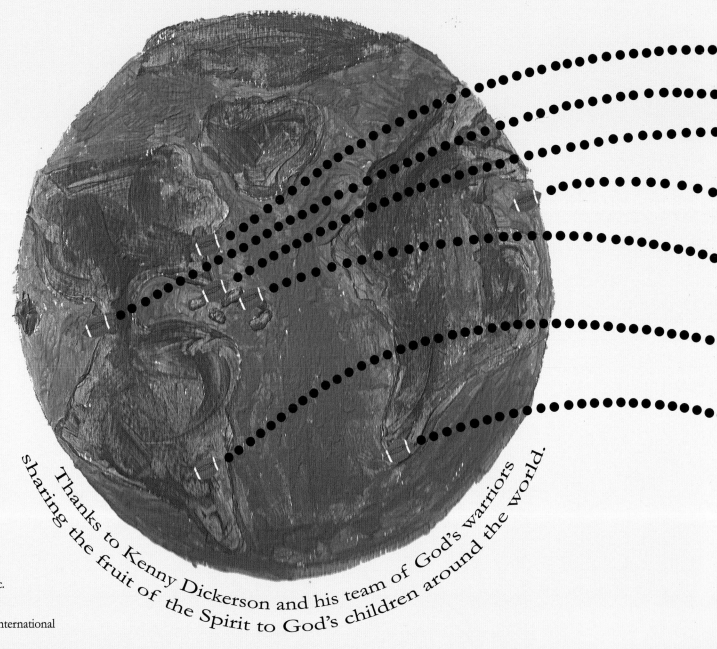

Thanks to Kenny Dickerson and his team of God's warriors sharing the fruit of the Spirit to God's children around the world.

Dr. Johnny Hunt
Pastor 1st Baptist Woodstock
(Former President for SBC)

Kenny Dickerson
President, Founder of SEAM, Inc.

Ron Bishop
President, Founder of SCORE, International

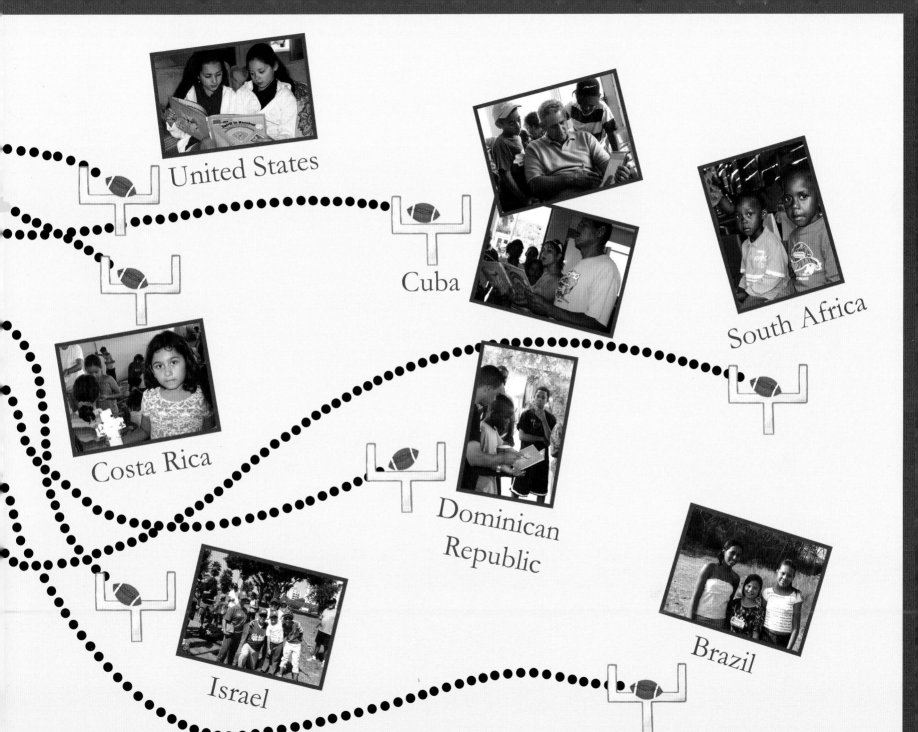

United States

Cuba

South Africa

Costa Rica

Dominican
Republic

Israel

Brazil

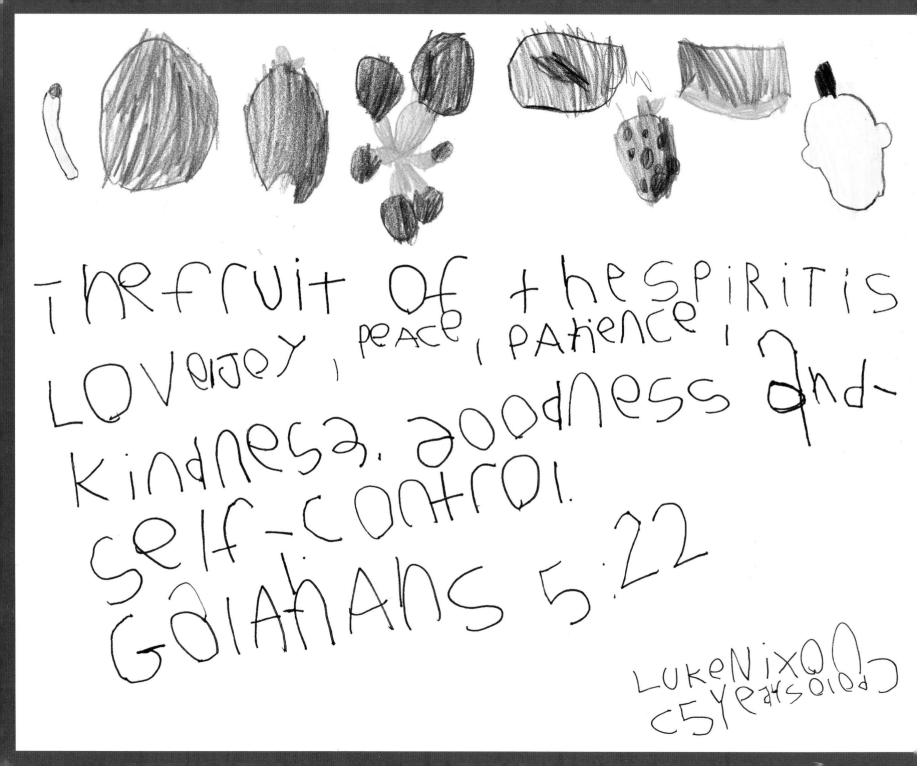

The fruit of the spirit is
Love, joy, peace, patience,
kindness, goodness and
self-control.
Galatians 5:22

Luke Nixon
5 years old

Love Joy Peace

Self-Control

Kindness

10 20 30 40 50 40 30 20 10

10 20 30 40 40 30 2010
50

Goodness Faithfulness Gentleness

About the Authors

Precious gifts of friendship....
knowing the heart of
another, sharing one's heart
with one another.
Author unknown

Kathryn & Ana

It was laid on our hearts by God to write and illustrate
together The Spirit in Baseball and The Spirit in Football.
We have been blessed by friendship and inspired by love to
share these books and God's message with you.
We hope you also feel the blessings of the fruit of the
Spirit as you share these books with your little athletes.

A Football Prayer

Dear Father in Heaven,

I praise and thank you for using the sport of football to draw me closer to You. I want to play this game so it is not about me, but all about You. I need Your Spirit to be in total control of my thoughts, actions, emotions and words. Help me not to worship the sport, but to be thankful for the skills and interests You have given me and to use them for Your glory. Help me also to encourage my teammates towards growth and maturity with You. Guide our coaches in making wise choices and help them be the kind of leaders You want them to be. Guide our parents and fans to support and encourage all players in the game with a cheerful heart and a voice of praise. Please keep all players free from injury, according to your will, and bring healing to those injured. Lord, I trust You to renew my strength in times of weakness so that You will be glorified in everything I do. Help me to praise You in victory and defeat. I love You and thank you for your love for us.

I pray these things in Jesus' name, Amen!

Written by:
Brent Coeling
Director of Kingdom Football Ministries